Top Skills

Writing Skills

For Selective Schools and
Scholarship Preparation

Therese Burgess

A
FIVE SENSES
PUBLICATION

To Max Jasper, whom I'm sure will be an inspired writer.

Five Senses Education Pty Ltd
2/195 Prospect Highway
Seven Hills 2147
New South Wales
Australia

Burgess, Therese,
Top Skills – Writing Skills

ISBN   978-1-74130-270-7

CONTENTS

Unit Number	Title	Page

INTRODUCTION

While **Top Skills: Writing Skills** is intended as an aid for Selective Schools and Scholarship exams, this book can be used productively by any upper primary student wishing to improve his or her written expression.

The book consists of 40 units of work. These cover the genres: description, narrative, procedure, explanation, exposition, discussion and review. As well, the units give practice in the areas which often create difficulty for young writers. These topics include –

- run-on sentences
- tenses of verbs
- subject-verb agreement
- correct use of person
- punctuation

Many exercises aim at improving the quality of writing by focussing on-

- more appropriate word choice
- use of detail
- 'showing rather than telling'
- practice in editing

Answers are provided for all of the skill-based exercises. Model answers are provided for most of the writing tasks. Lists of topics for the various text types are included. Students learn to write well by writing often. This book will provide the opportunity to do this.

Therese Burgess

*1. Use strong **adjectives** to exactly describe your characters in your stories. Choose the best **adjective** from the word bank to complete each sentence.*

generous	reliable	stubborn	bashful	amiable
elegant	diligent	gruff	loyal	moody

a. The detective regarded the young man as a _____ witness because his eyesight was very keen.

b. Susan is a _____ girl who loathes speaking in public.

c. My aunt always looks very _____ in her designer clothes.

d. A _____ student can count on doing well in exams.

e. The Senator was a _____ man who regularly gave large sums to charity.

f. We expect our friends to be _____ and not to reveal our secrets.

g. Mark can be very _____ and it is impossible to change his mind.

h. His friends become annoyed with him as he could be very _____.

i. Cassie is an _____ person who always has a smile on her face.

j. Grandpa can sometimes seem to be _____ but he is just a shy person.

*2. Use a **Thesaurus** to find three better words for the **underlined** word in each sentence. Your new words must **match** the ideas in the sentence.*

a. My aunt and uncle from California are <u>nice</u> people.

- _____
- _____
- _____

b. The visitors looked over new building which was very <u>big</u>.

- _____
- _____
- _____

c. Roland was given a severe punishment for a <u>small</u> error.

- _____
- _____
- _____

d. Victor felt relieved after he had finished his <u>hard</u> task.

- _____
- _____
- _____

e. "Mary is a <u>good</u> friend," commented Lucy.

- _____
- _____
- _____

f. They were tired after their <u>big</u> journey.

- _____
- _____
- _____

*1. A very common mistake in writing, is to change **tenses** of **verbs**. Verbs must be in the **same** tense. Rewrite these sentences so that all the verbs are in **past tense**.*

a. Humming to herself, Lucy brushed her hair and applies lightly perfumed lip gloss.

_____

_____

b. Edward was a frustrating person, and irritates his friends with his constantly changing moods.

_____

_____

c. I am sure that given a chance, the new worker would overcome his nervousness and prove to be a good choice.

_____

_____

d. The composer of this intriguing piece of music has no formal music training, but wrote many memorable songs.

_____

_____

e. Max enjoys chess but found it difficult to find an equal partner.

_____

_____

2. Choose a **stronger verb** from the word bank to complete each sentence.

regarded	examine	glared	glanced	surveyed
peer	witnessed	notice	gazed	glimpsed
spotted	studied	inspected	stared	watched

a. I tried desperately to _____ around Rose's shoulder.

b. Tom didn't _____ the cat sitting under his chair.

c. Carefully _____ the contract before you sign it.

d. Ellis _____ the arrogant new boy with open dislike.

e. The fan _____ at the rock star with fascination.

f. Alice _____ at the girl who made the unkind remark.

g. We _____ a serious car accident at that intersection.

h. The scientist _____ the virus under the microscope.

i. Mum _____ briefly at the note before signing it.

j. Last night, we _____ an absorbing television drama.

k. The detectives _____ the scene of the crime.

l. The explorers _____ the panorama before them.

m. The witnesses only _____ the mugger as he ran off.

n. I _____ at the exam question with mounting horror.

o. After an anxious night, we _____ the rescue helicopter.

*1. Choose the correctly **spelled** word in each set of brackets.*

a. If they make us a good offer for the car, we will (except / accept) it.

b. The school's dance item for the festival was (exiting / exciting).

c. Kassim has been given a new (bicycle / bycycle) for his birthday.

d. The (propellor / propeller) of the light plane was damaged.

e. Don't be (embarrassed / embarassed) when you have to speak in public.

f. The traffic was asked to (proceed / precede) slowly.

g. Divide the papers into two (seperate / separate) bundles.

h. We are doing a project on local (goverment / government).

i. My uncle, Frank, is a well-known (jeweler / jeweller).

j. You need to do this task (immediatly / immediately).

k. Make sure you include enough (infermation / information) in your report.

l. The boy was knocked (unconscious / unconsious) in the fall.

m. The spy tried to (dissapear / disappear) in the crowd.

n. The (mechinary / machinery) ground to a halt.

o. Were you (successfull / successful) in your entrance test?

2. Find the words in this section of a narrative which are **incorrectly spelled**, *and circle them. Rewrite the paragraph.*

The children woke early on the day of there hike. Quickly, they dressed, gathered together their equiptment and ate a hasty brekkfast of porrige and toast. Thay were bubbling over with exitement at the thought of the long-planed trip.

"Its a perfeck day for our excersion to the National Park," exclamed Luke, as they departed, waiving to they're mother. The wether was clear and fine, and their was no sine of a cloud in the sky. Paul, their teenage cusin, who was the leader, kept up a feirce pace but the others had no differculty keeping up. After two kilometers, they paused beside a streem for a briefe rest before resuiming their trekk.

_____

_____

_____

_____

_____

_____

_____

_____

_____

_____

_____

_____

_____

*1. All of these sentences need more **information** to make sense. Rewrite each sentence, adding either a **verb** or a **subject** (or both) to each one.*

a. At last, the prince back to his homeland once again.

_____

b. All night long, worried about the problem and did not sleep.

_____

c. Could not be sure about the best path to take on the hike.

_____

d. Into the dank cavern, the little band of travellers.

_____

e. Shouldn't have been there in the first place.

_____

f. Your goal, necessary for any chance of success.

_____

g. Struck the goal post and fell to one side.

_____

h. Across the park, my brother and his friends.

_____

*2. These sentences need to be **rearranged** so that they are more sensible. Rewrite each one.*

a. Deep in thought, the dog's sudden growl surprised him.

_____

b. Rushing into the room, a chair tripped me.

_____

c. Soaring across the sky, I saw an ultra-light aircraft.

_____

d. Hidden under a rock, I saw an interesting beetle.

_____

e. Stolen in the robbery, he found a bag of money.

_____

f. Borrowed by my sister, I feared my new top was lost.

_____

g. Abandoned in the rubbish tip, the boy found a gold ring.

_____

h. Eating a take-away meal, the unusual flavour surprised me.

_____

i. Sailing across the lake, the moon appeared huge to us.

_____

Complete the cloze with appropriate words of your own.
Draw a picture of yourself.

My name is _____
and my friends would say that I am
a _____ person.

I am _____ cm tall and I
weigh _____ kg. My hair
is _____ and my eyes
are _____ .

In my family there are _____ people. They are

_____.
My mother is a _____ and my father is a

_____ .

At school, my best subject is _____, but I feel that I
could improve in _____ and _____.
The best day of the week is _____ because

_____.

At the weekend, I like to _____

_____.

I think I am good at _____
and _____.
I am a good friend because _____

_____.

*Using the cloze as a pattern, write a **description** of a friend or of a member of your family.*

_____

_____

_____

_____

_____

_____

_____

_____

_____

_____

_____

_____

_____

_____

_____

_____

_____

_____

_____

_____

_____

_____

_____

_____

_____

_____

*Here are some more descriptions to practise. Remember to give lots of **details** to make your **description** interesting.*

PEOPLE:

- My Favourite Relative.

- My Oldest Relative.

- Someone I'd Like to Meet.

- A Person I Admire.

- My Teacher.

- My Mother.

- My Father.

- My Favourite Fictional Character, eg. Robin Hood.

- My Favourite Historical Character, eg. Julius Caesar.

- Myself as a Small Child.

- Myself in Ten Years' Time.

- An Alien.

- A Person Who Has Influenced Me.

- My Oldest Friend.

- My Newest Friend.

- A World Leader.

PLACES:

- My Home.

- My School.

- My Favourite Place.

- My Room.

- My Secret Place.

- A Crowded Shopping Mall.

- My Favourite Holiday Destination.

- A Deserted Street.

- A Small Country Town.

- A Circus Tent.

- The Beach in Winter.

OBJECTS:

- My Computer.

- My Most Precious Possession.

- A Battered Teddy Bear.

- My Favourite Item of Clothing.

- A Brand New Bicycle.

- An Old Piece of Sports Equipment.

- A Mystery Object.

*1. Use **adverbs** from the word bank to improve these sentences.*

extravagantly	copiously	impolitely	inconspicuously
contritely	peacefully	dishonourably	sadly
gruffly	unmistakably	smilingly	proudly

a.   The old man replied _____ to the questions.

b.   The boy answered _____ and was given a detention.

c.   The traitor was _____ discharged from the army.

d.   My aunt often spends quite _____ when she is shopping.

e.   The boy, guilty of shoplifting, apologised _____ to the manager.

f.   The water was flowing _____ from the burst pipe.

g.   I tried to blend _____ into the large crowd.

h.   The parents watched _____ as their son won.

i.   Carol looked _____ at her ruined skirt.

j.   The signature was _____ that of John.

k.   Despite the early problems, the day ended _____.

l.   "I really don't mind staying while you go," Sally replied _____.

                                               © Five Senses Education Pty Ltd

2. Use these **adverbs** in the cloze. Look up meanings in the **dictionary** if you are not sure.

restlessly	well	shrilly	suddenly
mockingly	apprehensively	slowly	sympathetically
apparently	probably	momentarily	sternly
vacantly	often	never	stupidly

The boy glanced _____ at the closed door of the Headmaster's office. _____Mr McWhirter was a very stern man, and not inclined to listen _____ to excuses made by students. Tom was afraid that this interview was not about to go _____.

Outside the window, a bird trilled _____ and a brisk wind whipped up leaves in the playground. Tom shifted his position _____ and realised that his hands were clammy. His eyelid was twitching and he held his hand to it, in an attempt to stop it, at least _____.

Across the room, Nicholas, his 'partner in crime' was staring _____ and tapping his foot. Tom asked himself how he could have allowed himself to become so _____ involved with one of the worst boys in the school. Nicholas was so _____ in trouble that he _____ wasn't in the least concerned about seeing the Headmaster.

The door opened _____ and Mr McWhirter appeared. Tom's heart-rate picked up and he felt a wave of nausea sweep over him. The Headmaster looked at him _____ and motioned him into his office. He glanced at Nicholas who seemed to look at him _____. Tom promised himself that he would _____ speak to the other boy again. Standing up, he walked _____ into the office. His legs shook so badly that he felt in danger of falling over.

*1. Each sentence contains at least one mistake in **punctuation**. Find it and correct it.*

a. I think Id better concentrate on perfecting my skills.

b. Robert, as captain, often raises his teams spirit.

c. Alanna a shy girl would not be a good choice as leader.

d. "Isnt Luke going on the excursion?" asked Brian.

e. The girls chosen are: Lucy, Amanda and Josie.

f. Please pack sleeping bags towels and spare clothes.

g. "Whose jacket is this," asked Mrs Walters.

h. Suddenly a roar erupted from the clump of bushes.

i. Joshua lives in Sanderson street, West Launceston.

j. We knew of course who had painted the signs.

k. It's obvious why hes a good choice as class captain.

l. The colours we need are blue yellow and black.

m. Explain the meaning of gruff.

n. The boss has left on four week's holiday.

o. We believe theyre likely to arrive soon.

p. The annual fete will be held on Sunday 5th April.

q. Luckily the bicycle sustained no damage in the accident.

r. It is likely that as a consequence he will lose his scholarship.

2. **Punctuate** this conversation correctly.

Alan where are you going called Reece as his friend came out of his front door

I have a meeting at one oclock replied Alan

Meeting What meeting asked Reece

I cant tell you said Alan beginning to hurry away

What spluttered Reece Im your best friend Why can't you tell me

Just mind your own business shouted Alan his face going dull red with rage I can have some secrets cant I

What do you think happens now? Write the next part of this story.

_____

_____

_____

_____

_____

_____

_____

_____

_____

_____

_____

1. *Replace* **'went'**, **'got'** *and* **'said'** *in each of these sentences with a* **better** *word.*

won	contracted	became	grew
retorted	spluttered	moaned	demanded
travelled	performed	returned	leapt

a. During the night, my brother's cough (got) _____ worse.

b. "Give it to me at once!" the shopkeeper (said) _____.

c. Our school band (went) _____very well in the state competition.

d. "I think I might have broken my leg," (said) _____ the girl.

e. Recently, my grandparents (went) _____ all around Australia.

f. I (got) _____ the 'flu when I was in the hospital.

g. "As if I care," the student (said) _____ rudely.

h. Tyler (got) _____ a prize in the spelling bee.

i. Pursued by the dog, the cat (went) _____ over the fence.

j. "But this one's mine," the confused man (said) _____.

k. The small children (got) _____ tired and cranky.

l. When the meeting was over, we (went) _____ home.

2. Rewrite this passage.

- *Replace '**got**' and '**went**' with words of your own.*
- *You may need to change words or add words of your own, eg. 'arrived **at**' instead of 'got **to**'.*

After we got to the camping grounds, we went to see the Warden to find out where our camp-site was. After we got to it, we got all of our gear from the van. Mr Nash put us into groups to set up our tents. This went well, and soon it all got done. Then, we went around meeting all the other campers. Most of them had got there a couple of hours before us. We told them that the traffic had got really bad and that we went at about 50 kmh for most of the trip. Soon, the hooter went, and we all got our hats and went down to the main assembly area to do craft activities. We had two hours for this and we got to do lots of different activities. After this, we went back to the camp-site and got our afternoon tea.

*Always **plan** your narrative before you begin. Think carefully what the **complication** will be, and how you will **resolve** it. Do not solve your **complication** by saying, "I woke up and it was all a dream!" This just shows the reader that you haven't thought out your story well. **Plan** this story.*

The Time Machine

Orientation:

Where will your story be set? _____
When will it be set? _____
Who will be in it? _____
How you know about or find the machine? _____
Why will you use the machine? _____

Complication:

Choose one:

[ ] There a problem with the machine.
[ ] The characters encounter danger.
[ ] The characters are asked for help by someone.
[ ] One of the characters needs help from the others.
[ ] A character becomes stranded.

Resolution:

Make brief notes on how you will resolve the complication.

_____

_____

*Using your **plan**, write the story. You may need to use more paper.*

_____

_____

_____

_____

_____

_____

_____

_____

_____

_____

_____

_____

_____

_____

_____

_____

_____

_____

_____

_____

_____

_____

_____

*Here are titles of **narratives** to practise.*

- Trapped in a Lift.

- It's Not Fair!

- The Mystery of Hollow Hill.

- An Unexpected Visitor.

- Success at Last!

- Lost in Space.

- A Voyage of Discovery.

- My Brother, the Inventor.

- Everything's Blue!

- Lost in the Labyrinth.

- Our Secret Hideout.

- The Enchanted Skateboard.

- The Tarantula Has Escaped!

- Snowed In.

- Pet School.

- The Missing Necklace.

- Don't Ask Me!

- Two Moons in the Sky.

*Sometimes, it is easier to write a story if you have the first line. Write **narratives** which begin in these ways.*

- The day began the way all Mondays begin, with the alarm ringing.

- Slowly, the massive oak door swung open.

- I love my sister, but sometimes she's a complete nuisance.

- There was a blinding flash of light and then all went dark.

- "Take me to your leader," croaked the alien.

- The moonlight made everything look ghostly.

- "It's time you woke up," said the cat, in a cheerful voice.

- How is it that some days, everything goes wrong?

- My heart raced and my hands shook.

- The box was of metal and tarnished with age.

- I can always rely on my friends.

- The small plane landed bumpily on the dirt airstrip.

- The footsteps came steadily closer.

- I looked down miserably at my wrecked bicycle.

- The only sound was the faint whistle of a train in the distance.

- It had been raining steadily for five days.

- There was a faint 'pop' and Jason disappeared.

- The huge metal doors closed with a hiss.

1. *Replace 'a lot of' in these sentences with a better word or phrase from the box. You may use items more than once.*

many	a great deal of	much	a number of
numerous	a great many	several	a crowd of

a. There has been (a lot of) _____ rain lately.

b. Our teacher gave us (a lot of) _____ homework.

c. (A lot of) _____ people gathered in the square.

d. The test was hard for (a lot of) _____ students.

e. We saw (a lot of) _____ tourists at the tower.

f. (A lot of) _____ students objected to the idea.

g. My brother has (a lot of) _____ hobbies.

h. You need (a lot of) _____ patience to play chess.

i. (A lot of) _____ students became sick at the camp.

j. I made (a lot of) _____ careless mistakes in the test.

k. You certainly have (a lot of) _____ CD's.

l. (A lot of) _____ supporters attended the game.

m. My brother doesn't need (a lot of) _____ sleep.

n. I read (a lot of) _____ books in the holidays.

2. *Three of the words in each line are* **synonyms***; one is not.* **Circle** *it.*

a. numerous   abundant   scarce   several

b. finally   initially   ultimately   eventually

c. later   thereafter   subsequently   sooner

d. travel   digest   roam   wander

e. solve   question   query   challenge

f. confuse   delight   confound   baffle

g. reply   reveal   retort   respond

h. obtain   gain   obstruct   acquire

i. object   article   item   odour

j. place   location   sight   site

3. *Find three* **synonyms** *of your own for each of these words.*

a. walk: _____

b. ask: _____

c. job: _____

d. look: _____

e. happy: _____

f. sad: _____

*1. Each sentence has **one** or **more** mistakes.*
- *Circle the mistake(s).*
- *Rewrite the sentence.*

a. I don't know were the box of coins are kept.

_____

b. There going to hawaii for their holidays in october.

_____

c. Take the peace of metal of the roadway.

_____

d. in Africa we saw lion's, leopards, zebras, and giraffes.

_____

e. Whose relatives are comeing for dinner.

_____

f. We allways go passed Rose street school each day.

_____

g. Jack as well as Tony are in the schools cricket team.

_____

h. The day was to hot so they stay at home reading.

_____

i. Lara, ben and myself attended the 2 day camp.

_____

j. The flock of sheep are hear near the house.

_____

*2. **Edit** this story.*

- *Check for errors in **spelling**, **punctuation** and **grammar**.*
- *Change the order of sentences if you wish.*
- *Combine short sentences.*
- *Take out words, or add them.*

William the Conquerer decided to build a fortress next to the Thames river. A wooden castle was already their. The fortress was began in 1078. It was finished in 1097. William has died by than. The fortress was cold and gloomy. It was built of stone. Kings did not enjoy living there, new accomodation was built nearby. This was a splendid and comfortable palace. The fortress was known as the White tower. Important prisoners were held there. A torcher chamber is maid in the basement. Later the fortress had been used for storeing arms and armour.

_____

_____

_____

_____

_____

_____

_____

_____

_____

_____

_____

_____

*1. Sentences can be written in many **different** ways.*

For example:
(i)   *The angry boy kicked the desk and hurt his toe.*
(ii)   *Kicking the desk, the angry boy hurt his toe.*
(iii)   *The angry boy hurt his toe because he kicked the desk.*

*Rewrite these sentences in **two** other ways.*

a. The dog chased the cat across the lawn and ran into a tree.

- _____

- _____

b. Dad drank a cup of tea and read the morning paper.

- _____

- _____

c. My sister stayed up too late and was very tired.

- _____

- _____

d. The wind blew down a tree and it fell on our backyard shed.

- _____

- _____

*2. Sentences may begin with **phrases**.*

For example:
(i)   *Our family held a birthday barbecue for Dad on Sunday.*
(ii)   *On Sunday, our family held a birthday barbecue for Dad.*

*Rewrite these sentences so that they begin with the **phrase**. A **comma** follows the phrase.*

a. Our whole family is always very busy on Saturday mornings.

_____

b. The wind blew the door shut with a loud bang.

_____

c. The full moon sailed across a cloud-studded sky.

_____

d. Not a sound could be heard in the packed examination hall.

_____

e. The lion sprang on the gazelle with a savage snarl.

_____

f. We are not sure where we want to go in the holidays.

_____

g. There are many computer games in my brother's room

_____

*1. Recounts need **time** words and phrases to show the **sequence** of events. Use all of the words in the box in the recount. Use each word **once**.*

Later	After a while	Soon	Before	Finally
Two hours later	Then	As soon as	As well	After

Last April, our family went to a town in the Snowy Mountains for a short holiday. _____ we left we had to pack the trailer with all the items we would need: food, clothes, games, sports equipment and the cat carrier for Tyson, our big orange cat. _____, we had to arrange for our neighbours to pick up our mail and papers, and to water the garden. _____, we were ready, and off we set in high spirits.

_____, we had left the city behind and were travelling down the freeway. In the paddocks were cows, and we saw some orchards and vineyards. _____, Dad said it was time for a break, so we stopped at a service station. _____ filling up the car with petrol, we had morning tea in the restaurant. _____ we returned to the car, we took Tyson out of his cat carrier and gave him a drink of water. _____, it was time to get on the road again.

The time passed quickly with some games and conversation. _____ , Dad said it was time for another break. When we returned to the car, we felt sleepy, so all of the children had a nap. We were woken by Dad's voice, saying, "We're here!" Our holiday had started.

*2. Write a **recount** about one of these topics. Remember to use good **time** words and phrases to show the **sequence** of events. Do **not** use '**then**' more than once.*

- A Surprising Event.

- The Day When Everything Went Wrong.

_____

_____

_____

_____

_____

_____

_____

_____

_____

_____

_____

_____

_____

_____

_____

_____

_____

_____

_____

Here are some more recounts to try.

- My School Camp.

- My Most Enjoyable Excursion.

- My Least Enjoyable Excursion.

- My First Trip Interstate.

- My First Trip Overseas.

- A Visit to Remember.

- The First Day of School.

- The First Time I ... (played tennis, had a violin lesson, etc)

- A Time I Became Lost.

- The First Time I Spoke in Public.

- My Best Birthday.

- I Succeeded...Finally!

- A Really Happy Day.

- When I Went To Hospital.

- When I Won a Prize.

- A Visit to the ...(Museum, Zoo, etc)

- When I Surprised Myself.

- A Wonderful Holiday.

*1. This is part of a very badly written **recount**. Rewrite it and change it in these ways:*

- *Use better '**time phrases**'.*
- *Make sure all the verbs are in **past tense**.*
- *Combine sentences using **conjunctions**.*
- *Use better words.*

Our class went to the Science Museum for an excursion. Our class went on Friday. We went by bus. The bus trip took an hour. When we got to the Museum we sat on the lawns. Then we ate our recess. We went into the museum. Mrs Ford put us in groups. Then the groups go to different places. The parent helpers go with different groups. The parents were Mrs Lewis, Mrs Chen, Mrs Hussein and Mr White. Then my group went to the Discovery Floor. We tried all the different machines such as the one that shows about centrifugal force. After we went to the Theatre and we saw a film about earthquakes. Then we went on the earthquake simulator. Jason said it makes him sick so then he tried to get off. Then Mr White told him to sit down.

_____

_____

_____

_____

_____

_____

_____

_____

_____

_____

_____

*1. Mark all the **mistakes** in this passage, and then write it out again. Look for mistakes in **grammar**, **spelling** and **punctuation**.*

Lucy was anoyed with her sister anna. anna has borrowed her new top without asking and loses it. Anna did'nt even appologise and just said to Lucy You have lots of tops but I havn't much tops. lucy has shouted at Anna than and has tore up her history project. She did not speaked to Anna after this, but Anna don't seem to care. There mother was upset with both of the girls and is giving them extra chores to show her disspleasure. She thort they should be ashamed of theirselves. Anna just sayed that she hadn't done nothing wrong.

_____

_____

_____

_____

_____

_____

_____

_____

_____

_____

_____

_____

_____

_____

*Have you been in a situation where you have damaged someone else's possession? Have you had a possession ruined by someone else? Write a **recount** of it.*

*1. Select a good **adjective** to complete each sentence.*

immature	considerate	foolish	cheerful
dejected	disrespectful	shocked	astonishing
hostile	trustworthy	deceitful	unpleasant

a. Alan's _____ manner always put me in a good mood.

b. To win the National Spelling Bee was an _____ feat.

c. We could see it was bad news from the _____

    faces of our parents.

d. Molly's soccer team was _____ after losing the Final.

e. A good employee must be hard-working and _____.

f. The salesperson was _____ in her manner, and so

    Grandma made a complaint.

g. It is _____ to leave your work until the last minute.

h. We hurried quickly past the _____ dog next door.

i. Lucy is always _____ of the needs of others.

j. That boy is much too _____ to be a good prefect.

k. Samantha's _____ manner earned her a detention.

l. A friend should never be _____.

*2. Sometimes young writers use **too many** adjectives. A few, well-chosen ones are best.*

- *Rewrite this paragraph, taking out some of the adjectives.*
- *You may combine sentences, or make any other improvements you wish.*

Sunday was a cold, blustery, miserable, freezing day. Max slumped in his hard, old, blue chair, staring at his computer. He felt ill, sick, upset and grumpy. His forehead was warm, hot and sweaty when he touched it. His throat was tight, sore and painful. He had a dreadful, sharp, severe headache. When he tried to concentrate on his interesting game, his vision was blurry and fuzzy. Finally, he gave up trying to play. He fell onto his snug, comfortable bed. He wrapped himself in his warm, cozy doona. After a while, he drifted off into a restless, unsettled, jumpy sleep full of horrible, frightening nightmares.

_____

_____

_____

_____

_____

_____

_____

_____

_____

_____

_____

_____

*1. **Verbs** must **agree** with their **subjects**. A singular subject needs a singular verb, and a plural subject needs a plural verb.*

- *Choose the correct verb in each set of brackets.*

a. The team of soccer players (has / have) eaten all the food.

b. My friends, Joe and Alice, (hope / hopes) to visit us this week.

_____

c. The huge, green troll (devour / devours) a great deal of meat.

_____

d. Each of the girls (train / trains) for three hours a day.

_____

e. Isaac, a friend of Luke, (was / were) involved in the trouble.

_____

f. Either Esther or Selina (learn / learns) Italian on Saturdays.

_____

g. The antics of the clown (has / have) captivated the audience.

_____

2. There are a number of mistakes with the **verbs** in this story. They may be in the **wrong tense**, or they may not **agree** with their **subjects**.

- *Rewrite the passage, correcting all the mistakes.*

Late one autumn evening, a young girl was walking to a well outside her village, when she seems to hear a bell ringing. This upset her so much that she slipped in the mud near the well, and fell down. When she has stood up again, she finds that everything around her had changed. There was no familiar trees or rocks and the well has completely vanished. Night has fell. Some distance away, a fire blazed and about it people are dancing. Looking closely, she realised that all the people are small, only about a meter high. The group stop dancing and were regarding her curiously. Nobody greets her. She felt very anxious.

_____

_____

_____

_____

_____

_____

_____

_____

_____

_____

_____

_____

_____

_____

1. Arrange these steps in **sequence***, so that they describe the* **procedure** *for making a sausage pie.*

[ ]   Slice up the sausages and arrange on the bottom sheet of

pastry.

[ ]   Beat four eggs together with salt and pepper. Pour gently

over the sausages in the dish.

[1]   Put six sausages in a pan and pour boiling water over them.

Leave until cool.

[ ]   Cut a 375g roll of puff pastry in half.   Roll half out and line a

square pie dish with it.

[ ]   Seal the edges of the pastry well. Prick the top with a fork.

[ ]   Bake the pie at 190 degrees Celsius for 45 minutes. Serve

hot or cold.

[ ]   Roll out the rest of the pastry to make a lid for the pie.

Place over the sausages.

[ ]   When they are cool, carefully peel the skin from the

sausages.

[ ]   The pie may be accompanied by a green salad.

Write a **procedure** for one of the following.

- *Cleaning up your room.*
- *Making a kite.*
- *Sending an email.*
- *Cleaning muddy soccer boots.*

Don't forget:
  - An aim.
  - A list of tools.
  - Numbered steps in sequence.

_____

_____

_____

_____

_____

_____

_____

_____

_____

_____

_____

_____

_____

_____

_____

_____

Use the information in the boxes to write a procedure on the opposite page.

How to Make a Bird Feeder.

Bird feeders can be made from a 2 Lt milk or juice container.

You need 60cm string to tie the feeder to a tree branch.

The two dowelling rods should be about 40cm in length.

Ask an adult to punch the holes for the dowels to go through. There should be a hole halfway along each side, near the bottom.

The container needs to be very clean.

The dowels are pushed through the holes. They make perches for the birds to sit on. The dowels should be at right angles to each other.

Four large 'windows' need to be cut in each side of the container. They should go down almost to the bottom of the container. Leave about 3cm between the bottom of the container and the window you have cut.

One end of the string is tied around the neck of the container. The other is tied to a branch of a tree.

*Write your **procedure** below. **Draw** a picture of your bird feeder.*

How to Make a Bird Feeder.

Materials: _____

_____

_____

_____

Method:

1. Clean _____

_____

_____

2. Cut _____

_____

_____

3. Make _____

_____

_____

4. Poke _____

_____

_____

5. Tie _____

_____

_____

*Try these **procedures**.*

- How to make a toasted sandwich.

- How to play "Pass the Parcel".

- How to play soccer.

- How to play "Snakes and Ladders".

- How to hold a party.

- How a train a dog.

- How to make an invisibility spell.

- How to make hot chocolate.

- How to mend a puncture in a bicycle tyre.

- How to tidy your messy room.

- How to study for a test.

- How to cook your favourite meal. (Ask Mum or Dad for help with this, if you need to.)

- How to drive a car.

- How to ride a skateboard.

- How to snorkel.

- How to reconcile with your friend after a quarrel.

- How to set up a fish tank.

- How to make a cup of tea.

- How to be healthy.

- How to swim freestyle.

- How to play "Hide and Seek".

- How to clean a car.

- How to juggle.

- How to do a load of laundry.

- How to play basketball.

- How to catch a fish.

- How to make pancakes.

- How to make a clay pot.

- How to make a new person to school feel welcome.

- How to tie shoe laces.

- How to train for a long road race such as the "City to Surf".

- How to make a model of the Harbour Bridge.

- Write directions for getting from your house to school.

- Write directions for getting from your house to your friend's house.

- Draw a map to find hidden treasure and write directions for finding it.

- Write directions for getting from your house to the airport.

- Tell how to train a cockroach in easy steps.

UNIT TWENTY-THREE   ADJECTIVES (3)

*1. It is easy to make mistakes when using **adjectives** to make **comparisons**.*

- *Choose the correct word in each set of brackets.*
- *When comparing two items, we use 'er' endings.*
- *When comparing three or more, we use 'est' endings.*

a. Does this book give a (clearer / clearest) explanation than that one?

b. Of all the projects, this one is clearly the (better / best) one.

c. My last assignment for this subject was the (more / most) difficult one I have done so far in the course.

d. Is today going to be (hotter / hottest) than yesterday?

e. After his dismal failure yesterday, Jon is a (sadder / saddest) boy today.

f. Of the twins, Daniel is the (taller / tallest).

g. Rachel is the (more / most) outgoing of the four girls in that family.

h. The townspeople were faced with the (graver / gravest) situation they had ever encountered in their history.

i. Your handwriting seems to be becoming (worse / worst)!

j. Are you (more / most) confident about your exam than you were last week?

k. Is the weather (more / most) unpredictable now than previously?

*2. Find the **mistake** in each sentence and circle it.*
   Rewrite the corrected sentence.

a. It is more hotter today than it was yesterday.

_____

b. Billy is the worse writer in the class.

_____

c. Sally made less mistakes than Annie.

_____

d. Max is the eldest of the two boys.

_____

e. This book is the better of the three.

_____

f. The storm was the worsest one this year.

_____

g. This drawing is more better than that one.

_____

h. Of Jon and Tim, Jon is the best musician.

_____

i. Were there less people at the game this week?

_____

*1. Rewrite these sentences in the **past tense**. The first one is done for you.*

a. I wake early, dress quickly and gobble my breakfast.

    I woke early, dressed quickly and gobbled my breakfast.

b. Are you certain that Fred is responsible for the breakage?

_____

c. Throughout the night, we rescue many people from the island.

_____

d. They have to bring our own food and utensils to the camp.

_____

e. We can see the smoke rising from a distant bushfire.

_____

f. Using a possum trap, the boys catch a huge feral cat.

_____

g. The people listen to the stirring music of the marching band.

_____

h. Is he aware that his brother has won the prize?

_____

2. This passage should all be in the **past tense**. Rewrite it correctly, changing all necessary **verbs.**

Jason was not sure what he was going to do. It seems such a good idea at the time. His brother was away at Wilderness Camp and leaves his mobile phone behind, because he was going to be out of range. So, Jason took the phone to school. Not because he wanted to make calls or to text anyone, but because the phone takes photos. He thought it would be fun to catch all of his friends unexpectedly! Besides, the phone has the best games and Jason imagines that he can quietly play them during Assembly. He just needs to make sure that Mr Simpson doesn't see him. Taking the phone seems like a good idea, but now he's lost it! What is he going to do?

_____

_____

_____

_____

_____

_____

_____

_____

_____

_____

_____

_____

_____

_____

_____

1. Sometimes, we forget who is telling the story. We might begin writing 'I' (1st person) and change to 'he' or 'she' (3rd person). We might begin by writing about someone else (3rd person) and change to writing about ourselves (1st person).

Rewrite this text to ensure it is all in 1st person.

I woke very early on my birthday and ran downstairs. I hoped so much that Mum and Dad had bought me a bike! Yes! There it was in the lounge-room, leaning against the sofa. Tim felt so excited and happy that he started to laugh out loud. My own bike at last! He had waited so long for it. Dad had been out of work for so long that it seemed I would never get a bike because there wasn't enough money. But, there it was in all its blue and silver glory. He couldn't wait to try it out and wheeled it quietly out the door. This had to be his best birthday ever!

_____

_____

_____

_____

_____

_____

_____

_____

_____

_____

_____

*The narrative you write in 1st **person** will be different from the one you write in 3rd **person**.*

- *In a 1st **person** narrative you can include your own thoughts and feelings.*
- *In a 3rd **person** narrative you can be the "all knowing" narrator and include other characters' thoughts and feelings.*
- *Write a short account of "**A Bad Day at School**" from both 1st and 3rd person perspective.*

(1st Person):

_____

_____

_____

_____

_____

_____

_____

(3rd Person):

_____

_____

_____

_____

_____

_____

_____

Which is best? Why?

_____

1. Match each proverb with its meaning.

Look before you leap.	Haste makes waste.	Charity begins at home.	Truth will out.
Don't cry over spilt milk.	Let sleeping dogs lie.	Every dog has its day.	Every cloud has a silver lining.

a. Don't stir up trouble:

b. Every situation has some good aspect:

c. Don't worry about unimportant things:

d. Don't rush or you'll make mistakes:

e. Don't act too hastily:

f. Everyone has a win sometimes:

g. Look after your own family first:

h. The truth will always be known eventually:

*Use one of the **proverbs** opposite as a stimulus for a **narrative**. Your story must demonstrate the meaning of the **proverb**.*

_____

_____

_____

_____

_____

_____

_____

_____

_____

_____

_____

_____

_____

_____

_____

_____

_____

_____

_____

_____

_____

_____

Use the information in the boxes as a basis for an **exposition**. *You may add more information, if you wish.*

WHY CHILDREN SHOULD DO CHORES.

Parents and children often argue about chores.	Sometimes children think they should be paid for doing chores.	When they grow up, children will need to know how to cook and clean.

A well-done chore can make you feel proud of yourself.

Every member of the family is responsible for keeping the house clean.

Your parents are not your servants.

Doing chores helps children become more responsible.

In many families, both parents work.

In some families, if a child doesn't do a chore, they are fined part of their pocket-money

A child who does not help in the home can become very selfish.

Your parents will be proud of you, if you help willingly.

     © *Five Senses Education Pty Ltd*

WHY CHILDREN SHOULD DO CHORES.

Introduction: (State your opinion clearly and strongly.)

_____

_____

_____

Point 1: (Give evidence for it.)

_____

_____

_____

_____

Point 2: (Give evidence.)

_____

_____

_____

_____

Point 3: (Give evidence.)

_____

_____

_____

_____

Conclusion: (Sum up your argument.)

_____

_____

_____

Complete these short paragraphs. *Remember to give* **evidence** *for your points.*

- If someone dared me to eat a worm I _____ because

_____

_____

_____

- I prefer to go to _____ for a holiday because

_____

_____

_____

- Something I will never do is to _____ because

_____

_____

_____

- I (like / dislike) wearing a uniform because _____

_____

_____

_____

- The best day of the week for me is _____ because

_____

_____

_____

*Here are some more **expositions** to practise.*

- Schools should teach driving skills.

- Smoking should be illegal.

- All boys should learn to cook.

- Homework has no value.

- Homework is very useful.

- The country is a better place to grow up than the city.

- The city is a better place to grow up than the country.

- Shopping is boring!

- Shopping is fun!

- Blue is better than red.

- Common sense is more important than being smart.

- Circuses should no longer have animal acts.

- School canteens should not sell junk food.

- It is better to be rich than to be famous.

- Cats are better pets than dogs,

- Dogs are better pets than cats.

- Some zoos and wildlife parks should be shut down.

- The driving age should be raised to twenty-one.

- Rats make the best pets.

*1. Match the correct **article** with each object or animal.
Remember these rules:*

- *Words beginning with a **vowel** have 'an'.*
- *All other words have 'a'.*
- *Words beginning with a **silent** 'h' have 'an' if the first sound we hear is a vowel sound, eg. an hour.*
- *Words beginning with a **long** 'u' sound have 'a' not 'an', eg. a union representative*

_____ error	_____ onion	_____ history
_____ head	_____ jetty	_____ insect
_____ expense	_____ extra	_____ apple
_____ update	_____ idea	_____ user
_____ flock	_____ donut	_____ glass
_____ usher	_____ union	_____ UV ray
_____ day	_____ canal	_____ oven
_____ alpaca	_____ batch	_____ whole
_____ matron	_____ investor	_____ itch
_____ husband	_____ pancake	_____ elder
_____ elm	_____ holiday	_____ cartoon
_____ fir	_____ honour	_____ end

*2. Choose the correct **article**. Think carefully about whether you need 'a', 'an', 'the' or <u>no</u> article at all.*

a. We decided to cook _____ appetising meal for Mum.

   [ ] the   [ ] a   [ ] an   [ ] ____ (no article)

b. The mother called the children to come to _____ dinner.

   [ ] the   [ ] a   [ ] an   [ ] _____

c. This is _____ unique specimen.

   [ ] the   [ ] a   [ ] an   [ ] _____

d. Has Dad finished with _____ morning paper?

   [ ] the   [ ] a   [ ] an   [ ] _____

e. We were confronted with _____ enormous elephant.

   [ ] the   [ ] a   [ ] an   [ ] _____

f. Brutus was _____ honourable man.

   [ ] the   [ ] a   [ ] an   [ ] _____

g. Would you like to have _____ meeting about this?

   [ ] the   [ ] a   [ ] an   [ ] _____

h. She asked me to have _____ lunch with her.

   [ ] the   [ ] a   [ ] an   [ ] _____

i. A good memory is _____ useful talent to possess.

   [ ] the   [ ] a   [ ] an   [ ] _____

1. Rewrite this conversation.

- *Take a **new** line for each new speaker.*
- *Add all necessary punctuation. You will need to put in commas, question marks, exclamation marks and inverted commas.*

Hi said Jay cheerfully. He threw his backpack on the floor and came to sit next to Max. Oh hello Jay replied his friend. What did you do at the weekend. Jay smiled and said I went fishing with my uncle. We had a great time. Did you catch many fish asked Max. No answered Jay I only caught one but Uncle Stuart caught five really good bream. Where did you go. We took my uncle's boat and anchored in the channel. That's where all the fish usually are said Jay. Max looked thoughtful. Do you think I might come with you next time you go fishing. Sure, replied Jay.

_____

_____

_____

_____

_____

_____

_____

_____

_____

_____

_____

_____

*2. Change these sentences which are in **direct speech** into **indirect speech**.*

Example: "Where is my backpack?" demanded Luke.
Luke demanded to know where his backpack was.

a. "Please help me with this maths problem," asked Jin.

_____

b. "When does the bus leave?" the young man asked.

_____

c. Neil asked, "Will you leave my books alone!"

_____

d. "This," explained Dad, "is the right spanner for the job."

_____

e. "Stop it!" yelled the little boy, as his brother teased him.

_____

f. "Are you sure," asked Mum, "that this is the right key?"

_____

g. "Has our visitor arrived yet?" asked Diane, as she came in.

_____

h. Rowan said, "I didn't get a good mark in the spelling test."

_____

1. Choose the correct **verb** in each set of brackets.

a. The lion, stalking its prey, (crouches / crouched) behind a clump of bushes and sniffed the air.

b. I saw a lyre-bird (ran / running) across the track when I was bushwalking.

c. He wasn't looking forward to the ferry trip because he always (becomes / became) sea-sick.

d. Luke knew that he should have asked before he (borrow / borrowed) the DVD, but he (chooses / chose) not to.

e. I could hear the throb of the helicopter rotor (increase / increasing) as it (comes / came) closer.

f. When we saw the tiny plane, we (feel / felt) nervous about the flight we (are / were) about to take.

g. A large group of people (gathering / had gathered) outside the theatre and (are / were) arguing loudly.

h. The crowd (press / presses) through the large doors, and (fill / fills) the auditorium.

i. I was often nervous about speaking in public and always (practise / practised) well beforehand.

2. Use the **strong verbs** from the box to improve each sentence.

surged	plummeted	shrieked	howled
snapped	stared	slammed	roared
collapsed	dimmed	lurched	plunged

a. The theatre lights (went down) _____ and the performance began.

b. The little red sports car (went down) _____ the street.

c. The boy (looked) _____ at his friend with shock.

d. The engine cut out and the plane (went) _____ towards the earth.

e. As the angry girl left the room, she (closed) _____ the door.

f. "Don't be impolite!" my mother (said) _____.

g. At the tragic news, the old lady (fell down) _____.

h. The speeding car suddenly left the road and (went) _____ over a cliff.

i. "Help!" (said) _____ the injured lady.

j. I (called out) _____ in pain as the paramedics moved my broken leg.

k. The battered old car (went) _____ over the bumpy road.

l. When the doors were opened at last, the crowd (went) _____ forward.

*1. Correct all the **mistakes** in this text. These include spelling, punctuation and grammar.*
***Finish** the story. You must **resolve** the **complication** in a believable way.*

"Look! Theres Alan" says Nick as they came into the playground. He pointed towards a thin red-haired boy sitting on a bench besides the library. They walk over to him. Alan looked up at there approach.
"Hey Alan, said Nick, I didn't thought you would be at school today. We heared that you were realy sick."
Yes, I was agreed Alan. "I had too go to Emergancy, and I stayed two days in the hospital. At first, I feel terrible, but than, suddenly, I started to get better. He looked seriously at his friends. "Can you keep a secret."
We nodded.
Alan continues. "Something very strange has happened to me. As I recovered, I relised that somethink about me were different. I think...I think...I've developed super powers!"
The boys looked at him with shock and disbeleif on they're faces.

_____

_____

_____

_____

_____

_____

_____

_____

_____

A **discussion** is structured differently to an **exposition**.

(i)   The question to be discussed is expressed in the introduction.

(ii)   Points for and against are presented.

(iii)   The conclusion expresses a decision for one side or the other.

- Use some of the ideas in the boxes to write a discussion.
- You may add ideas of your own.

Is Homework Necessary?

Arguments For.	**Arguments Against.**
• Homework helps understanding because it often goes over work done in school during the day.	• School is for learning; home should be for relaxation.
• Remembering to do your homework helps you to become more responsible.	• Homework is boring.
• Working on your own helps to develop your concentration.	• You should be able to learn all you need in school time.
• There is not enough time in the school day to get sufficient practice in the basics.	• If you have too much homework, you will not have time to play sport or get exercise.
• Homework may be boring but completing boring tasks without complaining makes you a stronger person.	• You are not learning anything new when you are doing homework.

*Use the **structure** to write a **discussion**.*

Introduction: _____

_____

_____

Point For: _____

_____

_____

_____

Point Against: _____

_____

_____

_____

Point For: _____

_____

_____

_____

Point Against: _____

_____

_____

_____

Conclusion: _____

_____

_____

*Write a sentence **for** the statement and a sentence **against** it. The first one is done to help you.*

1. Junk food has no value.

   ▪ _____

   ▪ _____

2. It is good to be an only child.

   ▪ _____

   ▪ _____

3. Guinea pigs make the best pets.

   ▪ _____

   ▪ _____

4. Engaging in extreme sports such as parachuting is foolish.

   ▪ _____

   ▪ _____

5. All children should play sport.

   ▪ _____

   ▪ _____

Here are some discussion topics to practise.

- Junk food has no value.

- It is good to be an only child.

- Guinea pigs make the best pets.

- Engaging in extreme sports such as parachuting is foolish.

- All children should play sport.

- All children should learn a foreign language at school.

- Intelligence is more important than beauty.

- Space exploration is a waste of money.

- Australians are too interested in sport.

- School hours should be shorter.

- Bike helmets should not be compulsory.

- Advertising on television should be banned.

- All zoos should be shut down.

- Mobile phones should be banned in public places, such as restaurants.

- The voting age should be lowered to sixteen.

- P-Plate drivers should have a night-time curfew.

- All students should complete Year Twelve.

- There should be more fun at school.

*1. Many young writers do not add enough **detail** to their writing and, as a result, it is not interesting. Compare these two sentences.*

(i)   The boys camped at the beach .

(ii)   Harry and Jack camped at Pebbly Beach for three days in the holidays.

Which is better? The second sentence is more interesting because it gives the reader more information.

- *Add the **detail** requested to each of these sentences.*

a. We went on a long holiday last year. *(Add where the holiday was and how long it was.)*

_____

_____

b. The boys won a contest at school. (Add the names of the boys and what kind of contest it was.)

_____

_____

c. We liked the animals at the zoo. *(Add the types of animals, the name of the zoo and when we went.)*

_____

_____

d. The excursion was fun. *(Add where and when the excursion was, and why it was fun.)*

_____

_____

e. We enjoyed a delicious meal. *(Add what the meal was and when you enjoyed it.)*

_____

_____

f. The boy was in trouble at school. *(Give the boy a name and say exactly why he was in trouble.)*

_____

_____

g. The car drove along the road to the beach. *(Add the colour and type of car, the kind of road (eg. bumpy) and the name of the beach.)*

_____

_____

h. I received a gift from my friend. *(Add what the gift was, when you received it (eg. Christmas) and the name of your friend.)*

_____

_____

i. The girls had a party. (Who, where, when and why.)

_____

_____

- *Organise the information in the boxes to write an explanation of how we digest our food.*

- *Use **present tense** and **technical language**.*

Teeth grind and cut up our food. Our saliva contains an enzyme which mixes with the food. It helps digestion.

Enzymes help to break our food down into useful substances which the blood can carry to the cells.

The oesophagus leads from the throat to the stomach.

The bile used in the small intestine comes from the liver.

The alimentary canal is a tube that begins at the mouth and ends at the rectum. All our food passes slowly through it.

The stomach makes strong movements which mix up the food with gastric juices. The juices contain pepsin, an enzyme.

The pancreas makes digestive juices used in the small intestine.

In the small intestine, blood and lymph vessels in the walls absorb the food particles. These substances are carried around the body to nourish the cells.

The large intestine receives the waste substances left over from digestion and these are expelled from the body.

HOW WE DIGEST OUR FOOD.

Introductory paragraph: _____

_____

_____

_____

Explanatory paragraphs: _____

_____

_____

_____

_____

_____

_____

_____

_____

_____

_____

_____

_____

_____

Conclusion: _____

_____

_____

_____

*This **explanation** is out of sequence. Number the paragraphs correctly.*

How is electricity produced and distributed?

[ ]   Substations receive the power carried by the overhead power lines. They reduce the voltage so that the electricity can be used in factories, offices and our homes.

[ ]   The cables connect to overhead power lines which are supported by pylons. The electricity carried by these lines is of very high voltage. The lines are insulated from the metal pylons by porcelain or glass insulators. Otherwise, the electricity would pass into the pylon.

[ ]   Electricity can be produced by harnessing the power of water, burning coal, geothermal energy or nuclear energy. It is produced in power stations by generators, and is transported away in large cables.

[ ]   In our homes, small cables carry the electricity through a fuse box into the wiring within the house. The fuse box protects our home from receiving too much electricity. If too much flows through it, the fuse melts and breaks the circuit, preventing a problem.

[ ]   When the electricity is carried to a big building, such as an office building, each floor or group of floors has its own supply.

[ ]   The lighting in a house is usually on a different circuit to that for stoves, televisions, etc. A meter measures how much electricity is used in the house.

     © Five Senses Education Pty Ltd

Here are some more explanations to **research** and write.

- How does a laser work?

- Why does it snow?

- Why do famines happen?

- How does a television work?

- How do we hear?

- What causes tsunamis?

- What work do our kidneys do?

- What happens when we breathe?

- Why do we have blood?

- How does solar heating work?

- What causes a rainbow?

- Why does it hail?

- How does a compass work?

- Why do we have seasons?

- Why do eclipses occur?

- What causes an earthquake?

- What causes a volcanic eruption?

- How do car brakes work?

- Why are there deserts?

*1. Excellent writers don't just **tell** something about the characters in their story, they **show** us.*

For example:

(i)   Sally felt nervous as she began her speech.
(ii)   Sally's heart thudded and her mouth was dry as she began her speech.

Which is better? The second sentence gives us a clear picture of how Sally was feeling.

- *Rewrite each of these "**telling**" sentences as "**showing**" sentences.*

a. Fred was furious with his mother for grounding him.

_____

_____

b. Alex ate messily.

_____

_____

c. Toby felt embarrassed as he walked into the meeting.

_____

_____

d. When the announcement was made, I was surprised.

_____

_____

e. When he saw the fire in the park, Daniel was shocked.

_____

_____

f. The wind was strong.

_____

_____

g. Rose looked very guilty as the teacher questioned her.

_____

_____

h. While Mum spoke to him, my brother continued to look defiant.

_____

_____

i. When Aaron received the news, he was very relieved.

_____

_____

j. The toddler was being difficult.

_____

_____

1. *Often, young writers add a weak adverb such as 'quickly' or 'slowly' to a verb and think that they have strengthened their writing. In fact, it is much better to use strong verbs.*

For example: She ran quickly to the door. (**WEAK**)

Compare with: She dashed to the door. (**STRONG**)

*Use a **strong verb** from the box to replace each **weak verb** and **adverb** in each sentence below.*

scuttled	charged	dawdled	crawled
crept	strolled	dashed	fled

a. The heavy traffic (went slowly) _____ along the street.

b. The enraged bull (ran quickly) _____ at the matador.

c. The tourists (walked slowly) _____ around the mall.

d. Hundreds of crabs (ran quickly) _____ over the sand.

e. The thief (walked slowly) _____ past the policeman.

f. The thief (ran quickly) _____ from the policeman.

g. The excited child (ran quickly) _____ from the room.

h. The girls (walked slowly) _____ on their way home.

*2. Check the meaning of each **strong verb**, then use each in a sentence of your own.*

a. (scurried) _____

_____

b. (peered) _____

_____

c. (slumped) _____

_____

d. (squinted) _____

_____

e. (bellowed) _____

_____

f. (slammed) _____

_____

g. (forbade) _____

_____

h. (gripped) _____

_____

i. (wrenched) _____

_____

*A review is a **description** of a book or a film which includes your **opinion** of it.*

- *Make notes about a book you have read recently.*
- *Use these **notes** to write a review of it on the opposite page.*

Title: _____

Summary of the plot: _____

_____

_____

_____

_____

What the characters are like: _____

_____

_____

_____

_____

Special aspects of the book, eg. illustrations, humour:

_____

_____

_____

Why you would, or would not, recommend the book:

_____

_____

*Write your **review** here.*

_____

_____

_____

_____

_____

_____

_____

_____

_____

_____

_____

_____

_____

_____

_____

_____

_____

_____

_____

_____

_____

_____

_____

ANSWERS

Unit 1: **1.**a. reliable b. bashful c. elegant d. diligent e. generous f. loyal g. stubborn h. moody i. amiable j. gruff **2.** Suitable words are – a. pleasant / charming / interesting b. massive / spacious / grand c. slight / unimportant / trivial d. difficult / tiring / lengthy e. loyal / dependable / reliable f. extensive / difficult / exciting

Unit 2: **1.** a. Humming to herself, Lucy brushed her hair and applied lightly perfumed lip gloss. b. Edward was a frustrating person and irritated his friends with his constantly changing moods. c. I was sure that given a chance, the new worker would overcome his nervousness and prove to be a good choice. d. The composer of this intriguing piece of music had no formal training but wrote many memorable songs. e. Max enjoyed chess but found it difficult to find an equal partner. **2.** a. peer b. notice c. examine d. regarded e. gazed f. glared g. witnessed h. studied i. glanced j. watched k. inspected l. surveyed m. glimpsed n. stared o. spotted

Unit 3: **1.** a. accept b. exciting c. bicycle d. propeller e. embarrassed f. proceed g. separate h. government i. jeweller j. immediately k. information l. unconscious m. disappear n. machinery o. successful

2. The children woke early on the day of **their** hike. Quickly, they dressed, gathered together their **equipment** and ate a hasty **breakfast** of **porridge** and toast. **They** were bubbling over with **excitement** at the thought of their long-**planned** trip,
"**It's** a **perfect** day for our **excursion** to the National Park," **exclaimed** Luke, as they departed, **waving** to **their** mother. The **weather** was clear and fine, and **there** was no **sign** of a cloud in the sky. Paul, their teenage **cousin**, who was the leader, kept up a **fierce** pace but the others had no **difficulty** keeping up. After two **kilometres**, they paused beside a **stream** for a **brief** rest before **resuming** their **trek**.

Unit 4: (Suggested answers) **1.** a. At last, the prince journeyed to his homeland once again. b. All night long, the old lady worried about the problem and did not sleep. c. The hikers could not be sure about the best path to take. d. Into the dark cavern, stumbled the little band of travellers. e. The foolish student shouldn't have been there in the first place. f. Setting your goal is necessary for any chance of success. g. The ball struck the goal post and fell to one side. h. Across the park, strolled my brother and his friends.

(Suggested answers.) **2.**a. Deep in thought, he was surprised by the dog's sudden growl. b. Rushing into the room, I tripped over a chair. c. I saw an ultra-light aircraft soaring across the sky. d. I saw an interesting beetle hidden under a rock. e. He found a bag of money which had been stolen in a robbery. f. I feared that my new top, borrowed by my sister, was lost. g. The boy found a gold ring abandoned in the rubbish tip. h. When I was eating a take-away meal the unusual flavour surprised me. i. As we were sailing across the lake, the moon appeared huge to us.

Unit 7: **1.**a. gruffly b. impolitely c. dishonourably d. extravagantly e. contritely f. copiously g. inconspicuously h. proudly i. sadly j. unmistakably k. peacefully l. smilingly
2. apprehensively, Apparently, sympathetically, well, shrilly, restlessly, momentarily, vacantly, stupidly, often, probably, suddenly, sternly, mockingly, never, slowly.

Unit 8: **1.** a. I think I'd better concentrate on perfecting my skills. b. Robert, as captain, often raises his team's spirit. c. Alanna, a shy girl, would not be a good choice as leader. d. "Isn't Luke going on the excursion?" asked Brian. e. The girls chosen are Lucy, Amand and Josie. f. Please pack sleeping bags, towels and spare clothes. g. "Whose jacket is this?" asked Mrs Walters. h. Suddenly, a roar erupted from the clump of bushes. i. Joshua lives in Sanderson Street, West Launceston. j. We knew, of course, who had painted the signs.

k. It's obvious why he's a good choice as class captain. l. The colours we need are blue, yellow and black. m. Explain the meaning of 'gruff'. n. The boss has left on four weeks' holiday. o. We believe they're likely to arrive soon. p. The annual fete will be held on Sunday, 5th April. q. Luckily, the bicycle sustained no damage in the accident. r. It is likely that, as a consequence, he will lose his scholarship.

2. "Alan, where are you going?" called Reece, as his friend came out of his front door.
"I have a meeting at one o'clock," replied Alan.
"Meeting? What meeting?" asked Reece.
"I can't tell you," said Alan, beginning to hurry away.
"What!" spluttered Reece. "I'm your best friend. Why can't you tell me?"
"Just mind your own business!" shouted Alan, his face going a dull red with rage. "I can have some secrets, can't I?"

Unit 9: **1.** a. became / grew b. demanded c. performed d. moaned e. travelled f. contracted g. retorted h. won i. leapt j. spluttered k. grew / became l. returned

2. (Suggested answer.) After we arrived at the camping grounds, we called in to see the Warden to find out where our camp-site was. After we found it, we unloaded all of our gear from the van. Mr Nash put us all into groups to set up our tents. This was a good system, and soon all was complete. Then, we wandered around meeting all the other campers. Most of them had arrived there a couple of hours before us. We told them that the traffic had been really bad and that we crawled at about 50 kmh for most of the trip. Soon, the hooter sounded, and we fetched our hats and hurried down to the main assembly area to do craft activities. We had two hours for this and we were able to do many different activities. After this, we returned to the camp-site and enjoyed our afternoon tea.

Unit 12: **1.** a. much / a great deal of b. much / a great deal of c. Many / A great many / A crowd of d. many / several / numerous / a great many e. a crowd of / many / a number of / numerous f. Many / A number of / A great many / Numerous g. numerous / many / a great many / a number of / several / numerous h. much / a great deal of i. Several / Many / A number of j. several / many / a number of / numerous k. many / a great many / numerous l. A crowd of / Many / A great many / Numerous m. much / a great deal of n. many / numerous / several / a number of / a great many   **2.** a. scarce b. initially c. sooner d. digest e. solve f. delight g. reveal h. obstruct i. odour j. sight

Unit 13: **1.** a. I don't know **where** the box of coins **is** kept. b. **They're** going to **Hawaii** for their holidays in **October**. c. Take the **piece** of metal **off** the roadway. d. In Africa**,** we saw **lions**, zebras and giraffes. e. Whose relatives are **coming** for dinner**?** f. We **always** go **past** Rose **Street School** each day. g. Jack**,** as well as Tony**,** **is** in the **school's** cricket team. h. The day was **too** hot so they **stayed** at home**,** reading. i. Lara, **Ben** and **I** attended the **two-day** camp. j. The flock of sheep **is here,** near the house.

2. (Suggested answer.) William the Conqueror decided to build a fortress next to the Thames River, although a wooden castle was already there. The fortress was begun in 1078 and finished in 1097, but William had died by then. The fortress, which was known as the White Tower, was cold and gloomy because it was built of stone. As Kings did not enjoy living there, new accommodation was built nearby. Important prisoners were held in the White Tower, and a torture chamber was made in the basement. Later, the fortress was used for storing arms and armour.

Unit 14: **1.**(Suggested answers.) a. Chasing the cat across the lawn, the dog ran into a tree. The dog ran into a tree because it was chasing the cat.   b. While reading the morning paper, Dad drank a cup of tea. Drinking a cup of tea, Dad read the morning paper. c. As a result of staying up too late, my sister was very tired. My sister was very tired because she stayed up too late. d. Blown down by the wind, a tree fell on our backyard shed. A tree fell on our backyard shed when the wind blew it down.

2. a. On Saturday mornings, our whole family is always very busy. b. With a loud bang, the wind blew the door shut. c. Across a cloud-studded sky, the full moon sailed. d. In the packed examination hall, not a sound could be heard. e. With a savage snarl, the lion sprang on the gazelle. f. In the holidays, we are not sure where we want to go. g. In my brother's room, there are many computer games.

Unit 15: **1.** Before / As well / Finally / Soon / Two hours later / After / As soon as / Then / Later / After a while

Unit 16: **1.** (Suggested answer.) On Friday, our class went to the Science Museum for an excursion. We travelled there by bus and the trip took an hour. When we arrived at the Museum, we sat on the lawns and ate our recess. Inside the Museum, Mrs Ford put us in groups which visited different places. The parents helpers, Mrs Lewis, Mrs Chen, Mrs Hussein and Mr White, accompanied the different groups. My group visited the Discovery Floor first. We tried all the different machines such as one that demonstrated centrifugal force. After this, we tried the earthquake simulator. Jason said that it made him sick so he tried to get off, but Mr White told him to sit down.

Unit 17: **1.** Lucy was **annoyed** with her sister, **Anna**. **Anna had** borrowed her new top without asking and **lost** it. Anna **didn't** even **apologise** and just said to Lucy, "You have lots of tops but I **haven't many** tops." **Lucy had** shouted at Anna **then** and **had** torn up her **History** project. She did not **speak** to Anna after this, but Anna **didn't** seem to care. **Their** mother was upset with both the girls and **gave** them extra chores to show her **displeasure**. She **thought** they should be ashamed of **themselves**. Anna just **said** that she hadn't done **anything** wrong.

Unit 18: **1.** a. cheerful b. astonishing c. shocked / dejected d. dejected / shocked e. trustworthy f. unpleasant g. foolish h. hostile i. considerate j. immature k. disrespectful l. deceitful

2. (Suggested answers.) Sunday was a cold, blustery day. Max slumped in his chair, staring at his computer. He felt ill and grumpy. His forehead was sweaty when he touched it, his throat was sore and he had a sharp headache. When he tried to concentrate on his game, his vision was blurry. Finally he gave up trying to play and fell onto his comfortable bed, wrapping himself in his cozy doona. After a while, he drifted off into a restless sleep full of horrible nightmares.

Unit 19: **1.** a. has b. hope c. devours d. trains e. was f. learns g. have

2. Late one autumn evening, a young girl was walking to a well outside her village, when she seemed to hear a bell ringing. This upset her so much that she slipped in the mud near the well, and fell down. When she stood up again, she found that everything around her had changed. There were no familiar trees or rocks and the well had completely vanished. Night had fallen. Some distance away, a fire blazed and about it people were dancing. Looking closely, she realised that all the people were small, only about a metre high. The group stopped dancing and were regarding her curiously. Nobody greeted her. She felt anxious.

Unit 20: **1.** The sequence is – 4, 5, 1, 2, 7, 8, 6, 3, 9.

2.   Aim: To clean muddy soccer boots.

        Materials: A stiff brush.
                    Old rags.
                    A bowl of warm, soapy water.

88   © *Five Senses Education Pty Ltd*

Polish.

Procedure:
1. Remove all loose mud and dirt with the stiff brush.
2. Wet a rag in the warm, soapy water and sponge off the mud.
3. Repeat until all the mud is removed.
4. Rub the boots with a dry rag.
5. When they are completely dry, polish the boots.

Unit 21: (Suggested answer.)

Aim: To build a simple bird feeder.

Materials: A 2 Lt milk or juice container.
　　　　　　Two dowelling rods, 40cm in length.
　　　　　　60cm of string.
　　　　　　Scissors.

Procedure:
1. Clean the container thoroughly.
2. Cut a large window in each side of the container. Leave about 3cm between the bottom of the window and the bottom of the container.
3. Make a hole halfway along each side, close to the bottom of the container. (It is a good idea to ask an adult to do this.)
4. Push a dowelling rod through the hole and out the opposite side. Push the other rod through at right angles.
5. Tie string around the neck of the container. Tie the other end of the string to a tree branch.

Unit 23: **1.** a. clearer b. best c. most d. hotter e. sadder f. taller g. most h. gravest i. worse j. more k. more **2.** a. It is hotter today than it was yesterday. b. Billy is the worst writer in the class. c. Sally made fewer mistakes than Annie. d. Max is the elder of the two boys. e. This book is the best of the three. f. The storm is the worst one this year. g. This drawing is better than that one. h. Of Jon and Tim, Jon is the better musician. i. Were there fewer people at the game this week?

Unit 24: **1.** b. Were you certain that Fred was responsible for the damage? c. Throughout the night, we rescued many people from the island. d. They had to bring their own food and utensils to the camp. e. We could see the smoke rising from the bushfire. f. Using a possum trap, the boys caught a huge feral cat. g. The people listened to the stirring music of the marching band. h. Was he aware that his brother had won the prize?

2. Jason was not sure what he was going to do. It had seemed such a good idea at the time. His brother was away at Wilderness Camp and had left his mobile phone behind, because he was going to be out of range. So, Jason took the phone to school. Not because he wanted to make calls or to text anyone, but because the phone took photos. He thought it would be fun to catch all of his friends unexpectedly! Besides, the phone had the best games and Jason imagined that he could quietly play them during Assembly. He just needed to make sure that Mr Simpson didn't see him. Taking the phone had seemed like a good idea, but now he'd lost it! What was he going to do?

Unit 25: I woke very early on my birthday and ran downstairs. I hoped so much that Mum and Dad had bought me a bike! Yes! There it was in the lounge-room, leaning against the sofa. I felt so excited and happy that I started to laugh out loud. My own bike at last! I had waited so long for it. Dad had been out of work for so long that it seemed I would never get a bike because there wasn't enough money. But, there it was in all its blue and silver glory. I couldn't wait to try it out and wheeled it quietly out the door. This had to be the best birthday ever!

Unit 26: **1.** a. Let sleeping dogs lie. b. Every cloud has a silver lining. c. Don't cry over spilt milk. d. Haste makes waste. e. Look before you leap. f. Every dog has its day. g. Charity begins at home. h. Truth will out.

2. It is important that the story doesn't just repeat the proverb, but actually shows what the proverb means.

Unit 27: (Suggested answer.)

Parents and children often argue over whether children should do chores. Children frequently dislike doing chores, and feel that they should be paid for doing them. However, there are several strong reasons why children should do chores.

Every member of the family is responsible for keeping the house clean because everyone lives in the house and contributes to the mess! In many families, both parents work, and as well your parents have the added responsibilities of cooking meals, driving you to school, taking you to after-school activities or helping you with your homework. Because your parents do so much for you, it does not mean that they are your servants! You should help with the chores.

Another strong reason for doing chores is that it prepares you for later life. If you never help to cook a meal or to clean the bathroom, you will have no idea of how to do it when you leave home.

Finally, if you do not help at home you may become very selfish, and always expect other people to do things for you. On the other hand, doing chores helps you to become more responsible.

No one likes doing chores, but if you do your chores well, you will feel proud of yourself. If you do your chores willingly, without grumbling, your parents will be proud of you too.

Unit 29: **1.** an error, a head, an expense, an update, a flock, an usher, a day, an alpaca, a matron, a husband, an elm, a fir, an onion, a jetty, an extra, an idea, a donut, a union, a canal, a batch, an investor, a pancake, a holiday, an honour, a history, an insect, an apple, a user, a glass, a UV ray, an oven, a whole, an itch, an elder, a cartoon, an end
2. a. a b. _____ c. a d. the e. an f. an g. a h. _____ i. a

Unit 30: **1.** "Hi," said Jay, cheerfully. He threw his backpack on the floor and came to sit next to Max.

"Oh. Hello, Jay," replied his friend. "What did you do at the weekend?"

Jason smiled and said, "I went fishing with my uncle. We had a great time!"

"Did you catch many fish?" asked Max.

"No," answered Jay, "I only caught one, but Uncle Stuart caught five really good bream."

"Where did you go?"

"We took my uncle's boat and anchored in the channel. That's where all the fish usually are," said Jay.

Max looked thoughtful. "Do you think I might come with you next time you go fishing?"

"Sure," replied Jay.

2. a. Jin asked for help with a maths problem. b. The young man asked when the bus left. c. Neil asked that his books be left alone. d. Dad explained that it was the right spanner for the job. e. As his brother teased him, the little boy shouted at his brother to stop. f. Mum asked if it was the right key. g. As she came in, Diane asked if our visitor had arrived yet. h. Rowan said that he hadn't got a good mark in the spelling test.

Unit 31: 1. a. crouched b. running c. became d. borrowed / chose e. increasing / came f. felt / were g. had gathered / were h. presses / fills i. practised
2. a. dimmed b. roared c. stared d. plummeted e. slammed f. snapped g. collapsed h. plunged i. shrieked j. howled k. lurched l. surged

Unit 32: "Look! There's Alan**,**" **said** Nick as they came into the playground. He pointed towards a thin**,** red-haired boy sitting on a bench **beside** the library. They **walked** over to him. Alan looked up at **their** approach.

"Hey, Alan," said Nick, **"**I didn't think you would be at school today. We **heard** that you were **really** sick."

"Yes, I was**,**" agreed Alan. "I had **to** go to **Emergency**, and I stayed two days in the hospital. At first, I **felt** terrible, but **then**, suddenly, I started to get better." He looked seriously at his friends. "Can you keep a secret**?**"

The boys nodded.

Alan **continued**. "Something very strange has happened to me. As I recovered, I **realised** that **something** about me **was** different. I think...I think...I've developed super powers!"

The boys looked at him with shock and **disbelief** on **their** faces.

Unit 33: (Suggested answer.)

Is homework a tiresome and boring waste of time, or is it a useful way of making sure that we really understand the work we do in class time?

Homework helps us to understand our school-work because it goes over what we learn during the day. There is no enough time in the school day to get sufficient practice in the basic skills.

On the other hand, we are in school for six hours a day and this should be enough time to learn all we need. Besides, homework is boring.

Yes, homework may be boring, but completing boring tasks makes us into stronger, more responsible people. As well, working on our own aids our concentration. If we work in a quiet place without the distractions of the classroom, we may understand our work better.

However, if we have too much homework, we will not have enough time to exercise. School should be for learning, and home for relaxation.

Homework may not be something we want to do, but it has many benefits for us. It helps us to understand our school-work more, to improve our concentration and to be more responsible.

Unit 35: 1. (Suggested answers.) a. In December last year, we went on a three weeks' holiday to the Gold Coast. b. Sam and Max won the Mega Spelling Contest at school last year. c. When we went to Taronga Zoo on Sunday, we liked seeing the giraffes and the red pandas. d. The excursion on Thursday to the Maritime Museum was interesting because we saw some old ships. e. We enjoyed a delicious meal of Thai curry last night. f. Brendan was in trouble for cheating in a test. g. The red Porsche drove along the winding road to Pebbly Beach. h. For my birthday, I received a CD of "Space Girls" from my friend, Vanessa. i. Lucy and Anna held a surprise party in a Thai restaurant for their mother on Friday night.

Unit 36: (Suggested answer.)

Digestion is a fairly long and complicated process with a number of steps in it. Our food passes from our mouth, though the stomach, the small intestine and the large intestine to the rectum where waste is expelled.

The first step is when the teeth grind up the food. Our saliva has enzymes in it which help with digestion and it mixes with the chewed up food. The food moves from the mouth down the oesophagus to the stomach.

In the stomach, strong movements mix up the food with the gastric juices. These juices contain an enzyme, pepsin. In the small intestine, bile from the liver and other digestive juices from the pancreas continue the process of digestion. Blood and lymph vessels in the walls of the small intestine absorb food particles and these substances are carried around the body to nourish the cells.

The remainder of the food passes from the small intestine to the large intestine. The waste passes down the large intestine to be expelled from the body.

Digestion is quite a long process, but every step is essential.

Unit 37: The sequence is – 3,2,1,4,6,5

Unit 38: 1. a. Fred's face was a dull, red colour and he muttered under his breath as his mother told him she was grounding him. b. Alex had food all around his mouth and splashes of sauce splattered the tablecloth. c. Tom blushed and hung his head as he walked into the meeting. d. When the announcement was made, my mouth dropped open. e. When he saw the fire in the park, Daniel gasped and turned pale. f. The wind blew branches off trees and ripped a roof off a shed in the park. g. Rose could not meet the teacher's eyes as he questioned her. h. While Mum spoke to him, my brother glared back at her. i. When Aaron received the news, he sighed audibly. j. The toddler threw himself down and drummed his heels on the floor.

Unit 39: 1. a. crawled b. charged c. strolled d. scuttled e. crept f. fled g. dashed h. dawdled